CW01573128

In Role

Materials for dramatic role-play and discussion for 13–16 year-olds

John Seely

Edward Arnold

© John Seely 1978

First published 1978
by Edward Arnold (Publishers) Ltd.,
41 Bedford Square, London WC1B 3DQ

Edward Arnold (Australia) Ptg Ltd.,
80 Waverley Road, Caulfield East
Victoria 3145, Australia

Reprinted 1979, 1982, 1985, 1987

All rights reserved. No part of this publication may be reproduced, stored in a retrieval system, or transmitted in any form or by any means, electronic, mechanical, photocopying, recording or otherwise, without the prior permission of Edward Arnold (Publishers) Ltd.

British Library Cataloguing in Publication Data

Seely, John
In role.
1. Drama in education 2. Improvisation (Acting)
I. Title
792′.07′12 PN3171

ISBN 0-7131-0295-0

Printed at The Bath Press, Avon

Contents

Introduction: How to Use This Book

The book is divided into seven sections. The first five sections follow the same pattern. Each one consists of the following:

The lead-in. This introduces the theme of the section by providing a number of quotations for thought and discussion. You can read and talk about these before starting work on the role-play situations, or you can keep discussion until later, when you have already worked through some of the situations.

Four role-play situations. These are for groups of 2, 4 or 5 members. The list of *characters* at the beginning of each will tell you how many. For these situations you are given two kinds of information: the general information on the page you are working on; and special information about each of the characters, at the end of the book. You should begin work by reading the whole description of the situation. Then do any necessary *organisation*; casting parts, arranging furniture and so on. Only when you have done all this, should you turn to the section at the back of the book, entitled *Roles*, to read about your particular character.

REMEMBER: *Read only your own character description. Do not discuss this with anyone else.*

When you have each had a chance to read and think about your role, then you can start the scene. You should begin from the moment described in the *starting point*.

The unfinished script. This is the beginning of a scripted scene for four or five characters. You can work on this in a number of ways.

1 You can read it individually, cast the parts in your group and then improvise the rest of the scene without any further discussion.
2 You can read it and then discuss it in your group before improvising the rest of the scene.
3 After a group discussion you can work together on writing a continuation of the script.

4 You can write such a continuation individually without discussion.
5 You can use your finished written script for acting out, or for recording as a 'radio' play.

The follow-up. This suggests in-role activities to follow each of the four role-play situations. It also contains topics for discussion after each situation. In addition there are suggestions of ways in which the unfinished script can be developed.

Section 6 of the book contains three longer and more complex role-play situations. In general these are similar to those in Sections 1 to 5, but extra instructions are included where necessary.

Section 7 contains separate instructions for nearly all the roles contained in Sections 1 to 6. As has already been pointed out, a lot of the value of the role-play situations will be lost if you read descriptions of roles other than the one you are working on, so please resist the temptation to 'snoop'. If you don't, you will probably find that later work is not so interesting or enjoyable — it would be like being told the ending of a mystery film or TV thriller before you see it.

Section 1
Me and My Family

Honour thy father and thy mother; that thy days may be long in the land which the Lord thy God giveth thee.

(*Prayer Book*: Ten Commandments)

All happy families resemble each other, each unhappy family is unhappy in its own way.

(Tolstoy: *Anna Karenina*)

Parents seem difficult to understand at times (about as often as they find their own children difficult to understand). What is often forgotten is just how quickly things change. How long ago is it since your parents were the age that you are now? What was life like then? Here is a man talking about his own childhood in Cumbria in the 1940s and comparing it with the present day.

'. . . You don't realise what sacrifices your parents might have been making just so you could have enough food and a new pair of shoes. I always felt I was one of the poor boys of the school or the town. I had to wear a pair of corduroy trousers which I didn't like, and I didn't like this. My mother would insist when I went to school I had to put clogs on which I used to hate at the time. But you see, my kids now, they're just the same. It doesn't matter what you give them, they don't like it . . .

'. . . I think people have more respect for children — what they're thinking — nowadays. We don't just say, unless we lose our temper, Oh, you'll do as I say. You tend more to talk to them, like grown-ups, whereas when we were kids if you didn't do as you were told you got a cuff across the lug and chucked out and upstairs or something. And you had to do as you were told . . .'

(Melvyn Bragg: *Speak for England*)

The Suitcase

Characters
A — Father/mother
B — Only son/daughter (your age)

Situation
A and B have not been getting on very well recently. It is about 9 o'clock one evening when A goes into B's room and finds B putting things into a suitcase. A cannot see exactly what B is doing because B hurriedly shuts the case and pushes it under the bed. B then stands up and is clearly very embarrassed.

Setting
A room with a bed, one chair, one entrance. Something to represent a suitcase.

Organisation
Cast the parts.
Arrange the working space as you want it.
Read your separate instructions, but do not discuss them.
A — 40
B — 12

Starting Point
B is kneeling by the suitcase, back to door.
A opens the door and walks in.

Football Fan

Characters
A — Son, aged 16, still at school
B — Father
C — Mother
D — Another member of the family

Situation
A is a keen supporter of the local First Division side. He goes to all their home matches and as many 'aways' as he can afford. (In fact he spends all the money he gets on football.) His father, B, is scornful of modern football with its

‘professional fouls’ and crowd violence, although in his youth he was a keen supporter of his local team. The mother, C, has never understood how it is that men can give so much of their spare time — and money — to a mere game.

After matches, A usually gets in by 8 pm for a late tea (unless it is an ‘away’). Recently he has been arriving home later and later. Today it was a home game, but although the time is nearly 11 pm, A is still not in.

Setting
The living room — armchairs, sofa, TV.

Organisation
Cast the parts (and decide on the character of D).
Arrange the working space as you want it.
Read your separate instructions, but do not discuss them.

A — **52**	B — **18**
C — **70**	D — none

Starting Point
It is just coming up to 11 pm. B, C and D are all sitting in the living room. A comes in.

Moment of Truth

Characters
A — Son/daughter, aged 21
B — Father
C — Mother
D — Son/daughter, aged 16

Situation
The family are fairly well-off. B is the manager of an insurance office and C is a secretary. D is in the fifth form at school and A has just finished a three-year degree course at Bristol University, studying French and German. While a student, A lived away from home during term time. A received a grant but also received money from B.

A is waiting for the final degree examination results to come. The whole family know that they are due any moment now.

Setting
Kitchen-dining room. A table and four chairs. A door leading to the passageway that goes to the front door.

Organisation
Cast the parts.
Arrange the working space.
Read your separate instructions, but do not discuss them.

A — 61 B — 32
C — 46 D — 4

Starting Point
All four are sitting round the table having breakfast. They hear the postman. A goes to the front door and comes back with one letter.

Time for a Change

Characters
A — Father/mother
B — Son/daughter

Situation
A is a widow or widower, retired. B is an only child of about 25. B has been very successful at work and this has meant making a number of moves from place to place about the country. The two of them have, however, never really lost touch and B has always visited A regularly at the family home on the outskirts of Coventry. For the past two years, B has been living and working in London and is very happy there. B is now in Coventry for long weekend with A.

Setting
The kitchen. A table and two chairs.

Organisation
Cast the parts.
Arrange your working space.
Read your separate instructions, but do not discuss them.
A — 56
B — 24

Starting Point
It is the Saturday morning. A has got up first and is getting the breakfast. B comes in.

Morning Delivery

Characters
Mother, Father, David (aged 13), Anne (aged 15).

Setting
It is 8.30 am on a Saturday morning. Mother, Father and Anne are sitting in the kitchen having breakfast. David comes in with the post. He has three letters.

DAVID Post.
ANNE Anything for me?
FATHER How many times have I told you not to talk with your mouth full?
DAVID No, they're all for Mum and Dad.
(*He hands two letters to Father and the other to Mother.*)
ANNE No one ever writes to me.
DAVID Well since you never write to anyone, it's not surprising really, is it?
ANNE Still, it'd be nice to get a letter.
MOTHER (*Holding letter which she has just opened*) Granny's coming to stay next week.
DAVID Oh no!
FATHER (*Warningly*) David!
MOTHER She says she'll catch the 9 o'clock coach and will we meet her at the bus station?
DAVID Mum — it's not fair! Every time she comes I have to give up my room.
MOTHER David! You should be glad to help out. After all she *is* your grandmother.
DAVID And she stays for ages — she's got loads of money. Why can't she stay in a hotel or something?
FATHER (*Holding letter he has just opened.*) I think this must be for you Anne.
ANNE Me?
FATHER Yes. We've both got the same initial, but this says

'Ms' and not 'Mr'.

ANNE (*To David*) Fat lot of use you are as a postman. (*To Father*) Can I have it then?

FATHER In a minute. It makes very interesting reading . . .

ANNE (*Suddenly realising what the letter is*) Please Dad — it's private.

DAVID Private? Who's writing you private letters then?

Follow-up Activities

The Suitcase

Writing in Role

A and B write personal diaries describing what happened in the scene, and their personal reactions to it.

Discussion Points

In your scene did A find out what B was really doing? How did A feel? Did the two of them get down to discussing their real problem? Did they reach any conclusion? Are misunderstandings and problems like this typical of most families — or can they be avoided?

Football Fan

Talking in Role

Pair conversations as follows.
A is put on probation and tells his probation officer about the family reaction.
When A has gone to bed, B and C discuss the whole business.
D tells a friend.

Discussion Points

How did A's parents react to what he had to tell them? Did their attitude change as the scene developed? What do you think a parent's attitude *should* be in such a situation? Do you think that in the end this will divide the family, or bring them together?

Moment of Truth

Writing in Role

Each member of the family writes a letter to a close friend, or relative, describing what happened and how he or she feels about it.

Discussion Points

Is A being selfish? How much should we expect from our parents? And for how long? What might the situation have been if A had learned that he had done very badly in his/her exams, instead of doing well? (*It might be interesting to improvise this second scene and observe how the different members of the family react.*)

Time for a Change

Talking in Role

Pair conversations as follows.
A tells the next-door neighbour (whom A knows very well) about what happened.
B tells a friend at work.

Discussion Points

Should B have told A of his/her plans before going so far? Should A have consulted B about the move? Why do you think they did not do so? Just how responsible should B feel towards A? What do you think will happen next?

Morning Delivery

In continuing the scene, you may find it helpful to consider these points.

What are the personalities of the members of the family, and what are their relationships? Which of the two topics of conversation (Granny's visit and Anne's mysterious letter) is the more interesting to develop? Should you try to keep both going at the same time? (David is, perhaps, more interested in Granny's visit and Anne in her letter.) How do the parents react? How do they feel about (a) Granny's visit and (b) the fact that their daughter is writing secret letters to people? And what is this 'private' letter about, anyway?

Section 2
Me and the Group

We all belong to many different groups. We have groups of friends, classes at school, groups we work with, even our family is a group we belong to. Some groups, like the family, are quite small and we meet them frequently. Other groups, like a class at school, are larger. Others again, like the football team, meet only from time to time.

Belonging to these different groups brings us different advantages. It is obvious that if you want to play football you must belong to a team. Other groups have less obvious advantages, but they are still there. Why does a particular group of friends enjoy going around together — to share pleasures, and problems; because they enjoy talking to each other; to help each other out? Think of a group of friends that you belong to yourself. What do you get out of it?

As well as getting something out of any group we belong to, we also have to put something in. Each group expects its members to behave in certain ways, and if we are selfish about this, we are soon told about it by the rest of the group. The selfish footballer, the lazy son, the 'friend' who lets the gang down — they all fail to put as much into their group as they have taken out.

Sometimes the different groups we belong to come into conflict. Perhaps our family disapprove of our friends, or our friends criticise the amount of time we spend with the football team. Then we have a problem of *loyalty*. Which of the groups is more important, and why? Sometimes such problems are very difficult to solve.

The situations in this section are all about belonging to groups. They concern problems such as loyalty, honesty, keeping your word and the conflict between different groups.

Promises, Promises

Characters

Five friends, A, B, C, D and E, who work in the same factory/

office. They are secretaries, clerks, packers in a large company that manufactures stationery.

Situation
This year the five of them have arranged to take their holidays at the same time. They have booked a motor launch on the Norfolk Broads. The holiday is to last two weeks. The launch was rather expensive and they have just managed to afford the cost equally divided between the five of them. The holiday is due to start on Monday. The group have arranged to meet during the midday break to make their final plans.

Setting
The works canteen. A table and five chairs.

Organisation
Cast the parts.
Arrange your working space.
Read your separate instructions but do not discuss them.

A — 7
B — 67
C — 22
D — 54
E — 67

Starting Point
It is the beginning of the break. As the five friends arrive, they collect their meals from the hatch and go and sit down at the table.

The Whole Truth

Characters
A, B, C, D are four friends who go around a lot together.
A and C have motorbikes.
B and D often ride pillion with them.

Situation
Today A has just got a brand new and very powerful machine, which he showed to the others with great pride. He left it in B's front garden, unlocked, when they all went home to have tea. When he came back after tea, he discovered the bike badly damaged, lying on its side in the middle of the road about

200 yards from B's house.
Important note: A and C have full driving licences. B and D haven't, although they have occasionally had an illegal ride on A's or C's bike.

Setting
The street. Something to represent the bike.

Organisation
Cast the parts.
Arrange your working space.
Read your separate instructions but do not discuss them.

A – 5	C – 34
B – 73	D – 15

Starting Point
A is standing by the wreck of the bike. Then B arrives, with a big plaster on his face. While they are talking, D arrives, and finally C.

Break-in

Characters
A, B, C, D and E are members of a youth club and are close friends.

A has always been the leader of the group, generally admired and respected by the rest.

Situation
A usually reaches the club before the rest of the group. Today when C, D and E arrive, they find he is not there, and nor is Dave, a popular member of the group. They discover that several windows have been smashed. Then B arrives with some news.

Setting
The youth club building. There are two doors: one leading to the outside and the other to the club leader's room.

Organisation
Cast the parts.
Arrange your working area. Now A should go out of earshot

for the first part of the scene, so that he/she does not know what is going on, but in the direction that you have decided the leader's room is.
Now read your separate instructions but do not discuss them.

A — 10
B — 69
C — 42
D — 27
E — 27

Starting Point
C, D and E are in the club room looking at the damage. B comes in and starts talking to them.

Who's Your Friend?

Characters
A — boy or girl, aged about 15
B, C — two of A's friends
D — A's mother or father

Situation
A, B, and C often meet up on Saturday mornings, at the Black and White Cafe in the centre of town. This Saturday morning is no exception.

Setting
A cafe — one table and four chairs.

Organisation
Cast the parts.
Arrange the working space.
Read your separate instructions, but do not discuss them.
A — 13
B/C — 65
D — 49

Starting Point
B and C are sitting talking in the cafe.
A comes in and joins them.
Note: If possible, D should not listen to their conversation, until the moment comes to join in the scene.

Better Late Than Never

Characters and Setting

Four teenage friends, Kevin, Pat, Jay and Mike are on holiday together at Butlins. It is 9.30 am and Jay, Pat and Mike are waiting for Kevin, who is late.

JAY Here he comes.
PAT Late — as usual.
MIKE He'd better have a good reason.
(Kevin arrives. He is cheerful and at ease.)
KEVIN Hullo, Jay, Pat. Hi Mike.
JAY Hallo.
MIKE Where were you?
KEVIN Hallo Mike.
MIKE I said where were you?
KEVIN Yes, I heard you. And I said Hallo Mike.
MIKE Don't you start coming the acid —
KEVIN I'm not. I just thought it'd be nice to be polite, that's all.
JAY Hark at him! (*Imitation 'posh' voice*) Fraitfully naice to meet you, Aim sure!
MIKE I want to know where you were.
KEVIN When?
MIKE Last night, of course. 8 o'clock we said. We were all waiting here, bang on eight and you didn't show up.
PAT Yes — we waited till nearly half past.
MIKE So we missed the film. Where were you?
JAY Yeah. Come on Kevin — why didn't you turn up?
KEVIN Yes, well, I'm sorry about that. I couldn't make it.
MIKE What do you mean 'couldn't make it'? *Why* couldn't you make it?
KEVIN I'm sorry. I just couldn't — that's all.
MIKE Why not? Were not at home — we're at Butlins. What was there to stop you? Come on Kevin, We're not fooling around you know. You messed up our evening —

Follow-up Activities

Promises, Promises

Talking in Role

As a result of the conversation, all the members of the group are late returning to work. Each has to explain to a curious and suspicious boss/foreman *why* he or she was late.

Discussion Points

How did your scene end? What decision was reached? Do you now think it was the right one? What are the rights and wrongs of situations like this?

The Whole Truth

Improvisation Situation

Just as the original scene is ending, a policeman comes along and wants to know what has been going on.

Discussion Points

Begin your discussion by telling the rest of the group exactly what your separate instructions said. Did each character tell 'the whole truth'? What can A now tell the owner of the bike? Should he involve D? What part did B and C play in the scene? Did they help, or hinder?

Break-ins

Talking in Role

Each member of the group talks to Dave and tells him what happened at the youth club.

Discussion Points

Do you think that the others would really talk about A behind his back? Is it fair to do that? Should people *always* tell others of their opinion about them to their faces, even when they are very critical? What do *you* do?

Who's Your Friend?

Talking in Role

A and D talk again, at home, about what happened.
B/C — each discusses it with a parent.

Discussion Points
How often does this kind of conflict happen? What rights do parents have to make rules about their sons' and daughters' friends? What rights have the sons and daughters got to go around with whom they please? How is this affected by your age?

Better Late Than Never

Some Points to Think About
What are the characters and relationships of the four people? Who is the leader? How much does the leader dominate the rest of the group? Why did Kevin not turn up last night? Why is he unwilling to explain to the others? Does he explain in the end? How do the others react? Are they sympathetic, or hostile? How does the scene end?

Section 3
Me and My Friends

Life is nothing without friendship.

(Cicero)

Most friendship is feigning, most loving mere folly.

(Shakespeare)

Greater love hath no man than this, that a man lay down his life for his friends.

(*The Bible*)

How many friends have you got? Not just acquaintances, people you go around with or meet at school every day, but *friends*? What do you mean when you call someone a 'friend'? Is it really true that life is nothing without friendship? Or could you in fact get along perfectly well without your friends?

Friendship can lead to conflict. Sometimes it leads to conflict with parents. They may feel that a certain friend is 'unsuitable', as happens in *Who's Your Friend?* in the previous section. Then, too, we may find that there is a conflict *inside* us between a friendship and something we believe in very strongly. What is more important: the friend or the principle? One of the situations in this section deals with just such a conflict.

You have probably heard that quotation from the Bible a thousand times before. But what does it mean? Just how much would *you* be prepared to give up for a friend? Or is most friendship just feigning, pretending, as Shakespeare says?

Just a Loan

Characters
A and B, two friends.

Situation
A and B have been friends for a long time. They often go around together and last year B went on holiday with A and

A's family. They have not seen quite as much of each other recently, though.

Setting
A classroom. Two chairs for A and B to sit on if they wish. It is the midday break.

Organisation
Cast the parts.
Arrange the working space.
Read your separate instructions but do not discuss them.
A — **16**
B — **59**

Starting Point
B is sitting alone in the classroom and A comes in. A wants to talk to B, but there isn't much time before the bell goes for afternoon school.

Finders ... Keepers?

Characters
A and B are two close friends. A's father is a police sergeant. B's father is a businessman, whose firm has recently gone bankrupt. B's father is therefore unemployed.

Situation
A and B have been collecting old clothes for a school jumble sale. When they get back to the school that evening they start sorting out the clothes they have collected. In the pocket of an old jacket B finds an envelope containing nearly fifteen pounds in dirty banknotes. Both A and B can remember who gave them the jacket — an old man who lives all alone in a very big house not far from the school.

Setting
A school classroom in which the desks have been put together to take all the old clothes. It is evening and there is no one else in the room.

Organisation
Cast the parts.
Arrange your working space.
Read your separate instructions but do not discuss them.
A — 30
B — 74

Starting Point
A and B are sorting the clothes. B finds the envelope and opens it.

Priorities

Characters
A — boy, still at school and just going into sixth form. His parents have never said much about his going around with B.
B — girlfriend, who has just left school to do a commercial course at the local college.

Situation
A and B have been going out together for some time. B's parents approve of A and he has visited her home a number of times. On this occasion A and B have a date to go to the pictures.

Setting
Just outside the cinema.

Organisation
Cast the parts.
Read your separate instructions, but do not discuss them.
A — 17
B — 63

Starting Point
B is waiting outside the cinema. It is two minutes before the film is due to begin. A is ten minutes late, which is unusual for him. Then he arrives.

The Babysitter

Characters
A — Boy or girl of about 15. The only son, or daughter of B.
B — Mother or father. A widow or widower.

Situation
A and B have developed a very close relationship over the past three years and B has always thought that there were no secrets between them. Just recently, however, A has wanted more time to himself/herself and has found B rather inquisitive. B has found A secretive. Recently A has been out babysitting on a number of evenings. On this occasion, A has been out babysitting again. It is 11 pm when he/she returns.

Setting
Their living room. Easy chairs and a TV.

Organisation
Cast the parts.
Arrange the working area.
Read your separate instructions, but do not discuss them.
A — 21
B — 55

Starting Point
B is sitting watching TV. A comes into the room.

Confrontation

Tom is about 16. He lives in a caravan with his parents. His girlfriend Jan is there one Sunday evening when Tom's parents ask to speak to the two of them.

Jan led the way to the other end of the caravan. Tom's father turned off the volume control on the television.

'It must be serious,' said Tom.

'Shut up,' said Jan.

'Sit down: will you — please? On the divan.'

They sat. Tom's father went to the window and peered out half facing the room, his hands behind his back. 'Stand easy,' said Tom. His mother lodged one buttock on the arm of a chair, swinging her foot.

'I want to ask — '

'What'?

'I want to ask you and Jan — '

'What?'

'It's written all over you,' said his mother.

'Your mother and I would like to know whether you've anything to tell us.'

'What's your problem?' Tom reached out his hand for Jan. She took it.

'We think — '

'Both of you?'

'Don't,' said Jan.

'I'm trying to be useful,' said Tom.

'Like hell.'

'Watch that tongue of yours!' said Tom's mother.

'She'd look pretty silly if she did.'

'Stop arsing around,' Jan whispered.

'I heard that!'

'Let's try again,' his father said.

Tom opened his mouth, but Jan kicked him.

'Your mother and I. We wondered if you'd any occasion to do anything to make us ashamed of you.'

Red Shift by Alan Garner

Follow-up Activities

Just a Loan

Pair Improvisation

Suppose that B will only lend the money on condition that he/she has the spare ticket. A now has to explain this to the friend to whom he/she had promised that ticket.

Discussion Points

The old saying is *Neither a borrower nor a lender be.* What is your opinion?

Finders . . . Keepers?

Talking in Role

A tells his/her father about what happened.
B tells his/her mother.

Discussion Points

What would you have done in real life if you had been B? Is A's attitude true to life? Is it reasonable?

Priorities

Writing in Role

A writes a letter to a close friend describing what happened and how he feels about it.
B writes an account of it in her personal diary.

Discussion Points

Do you think A's parents are right? If you were A, would you have accepted what they said? How far should parents go in advising their sons and daughters about their friends? How would *you* deal with this kind of situation if you were a parent?

The Babysitter

Writing in Role

A writes a letter to the girlfriend/boyfriend telling him/her what happened and explaining how it will affect them.
B writes a letter to a close friend of B's own age telling him/her what happened.

Discussion Points

Was A right to pretend in this way? What would you have done in this situation? How did B react in your scene? Was this the best way to handle it? If not, what should B have done? What do you think should happen now?

Confrontation

Although this scene is in the form of a conversation from a novel, it can be developed in exactly the same way as the short scripts in the last two sections. You may find it helps you to begin by writing it down as a script. For example:

TOM	It must be serious.
JAN	Shut up.
FATHER	Sit down: will you — please. On the divan. (*Tom and Jan sit down. Father stands by the window.*)

and so on.

Section 4
Me and Other People

Suppose you are out somewhere with friends and you meet someone you have never met before: how do you make up your mind what kind of person he or she is?

Some people judge others by the clothes they wear and their hairstyle. Long hair and jeans means a student; grey suit and briefcase means an office worker. It is true that people in many different walks of life wear a kind of uniform, but does this tell us what kind of person is wearing the uniform? You may well be wearing a school uniform, but it does not tell anyone very much about *you*. Still, many people are influenced in their opinions of others by the clothes other people wear.

Others may be guided by the way in which a person behaves, particularly if this is very different from what they are used to. We tend to think that if people do not do things the way we do, they must be odd or unusual, as if *our* behaviour is 'normal' or even 'the best'.

How you speak (and what you say) certainly affects the judgements people will make about you. When you apply for a job, for example, you may well have an interview. The interviewer has to decide whether to give you the job on the basis of how you answer his questions. Both the words you speak and the way in which you speak them will help him to make up his mind . . . one way or the other.

When we are forming opinions about people, one of the things we decide about is how far we can *trust* the person we are talking to. Is he or she truthful and sincere? Can he or she be relied on? These are important questions that affect the way we behave with people we do not know well. If we decide that the answer to these questions is 'yes', then the relationship can develop. If it is 'no', then we remain cautious and wary.

Each scene in this section concerns an encounter between strangers.

The Traveller

Characters

A, B, C — three middle-aged people, who come from the same area and know each other by sight, but not to talk to.

D — a young man wearing jeans and carrying a pack, a stranger to the area.

Situation

It is quite late at night. A, B and C are sitting in a cafe next door to the bus station, waiting for the last bus, which is due to leave in about five minutes. It is a cold, wet night.

Setting

The cafe. Tables and chairs.

Organisation

Cast the parts.
Arrange the working space.
Read your separate instructions, but do not discuss them.

A — 1	C — 71
B — 71	D — 29

Starting Point

A, B, C are sitting in the cafe. D walks in, soaking wet.

Good Neighbours

Characters

A — Mr Selby, an office worker
B — Mrs Selby
C — David, their son, aged 18. He is still at school, but leaving shortly
D — Reuben Lee, their next-door neighbour
E — Maria, aged 17, his daughter

Situation

The Selby family have lived in their semidetached house in a quiet suburb for many years. Recently some new neighbours moved in, Reuben Lee and his daughter Maria. It soon became clear that the two families have very different ways of life. The Selbys like to keep themselves to themselves and pride themselves on the neatness and cleanness of their house and garden. The Lees like company and there always seems to be a party going on in their house, with people coming and going until the small hours. In addition Reuben Lee appears to collect motor car engines and there are always several old cars in various stages of disintegration laying about his garden, which is now overgrown with weeds.

Setting
The two gardens, with the fence running between them. Two chairs in the Selbys' garden.

Organisation
Cast the parts.
Arrange your working space and make sure that you know where the fence is.
Read your separate instructions but do not discuss them.

A — **8**
B — **60**
C — **39**
D — **51**
E — **75**

Starting Point
It is a warm summer evening and Mr and Mrs Selby are sitting relaxing in their garden when Mr Lee next door starts hammering away at one of his engines, making a very loud noise indeed. At that moment, David Selby comes into the garden.

Interview

Characters
A — Managing Director of Partysound Records
B — Personnel Manager of Partysound
C/D — two applicants for the job of Assistant to the Personnel Manager

Situation
Partysound is a large record company specialising in pop music. The employees of the firm are very well paid and there has been a lot of competition for the post of Assistant

Personnel Manager. Now it is between these two applicants, C and D.

Setting
The large room being used for interviews. A table with two chairs on one side of it and one on the other.

Organisation
Cast the parts.
Arrange your working space.
Read your separate instructions, but do not discuss them.

A — **19**	C — **26**
B — **57**	D — **68**

Starting Point
A and B are sitting in the interview room before the interviews begin. C and D should sit so that they cannot hear what is said in the interview room. A and B discuss what they are looking for in the applicants. When they are ready, they will call for C to come in.

Note
After both C and D have been interviewed, A and B should decide whom to appoint.

It's a Secret

Characters
A — Peter Hargreaves, a soldier who has just come home on leave
B — Mary, his fiancee
C — His mother or father
D — A reporter from the local paper

Situation
Peter has just returned from a tour of duty in Belfast. He has said that his work there is secret, but Mary believes that he has been working for an undercover unit on some kind of dangerous and difficult work. He has only just come home and is sitting talking to B and C when there is a knock at the door. It is a reporter from the local paper who would like to interview him.

Setting
The living room. Four chairs.

Organisation
Cast the parts.
Arrange the working area.
Read your separate instructions, but do not discuss them.

A — 14	C — 33
B — 64	D — 53

Starting Point
A, B and C are talking when there is a knock at the door. C goes to see who it is and comes back with D.

The New Boy

Setting
An ordinary classroom in a school like yours. It is first thing in the morning and the teacher, Mr Robinson, has just finished calling the register.

MR ROBINSON	Williams.
DAVE	Present.
MR ROBINSON	Now then, there's something I want to tell you. We've got a new boy joining the class today. His name is Terrett and I want you to make sure that he is made welcome. Gary —
GARY	Yes Mr Robinson?
MR ROBINSON	You keep an eye on him, will you? Find him a locker, make sure he gets the right books and so on.
GARY	Yes.
MR ROBINSON	Good. Get your books out for the first lesson. (*He goes out.*)
BRIAN	(*Imitating*) 'I want you to make sure that he is made welcome.' What are we supposed to do, put down a red carpet?
GARY	Oh go on, Brian, you know what he means.
JANE	Brian couldn't make anyone welcome if he tried.

DAVE No — his idea of a welcome is to trip you up and stand on —

BRIAN (*Going across to Dave*) On what?

DAVE His dignity of course, Brian — what did you think I was going to say? Except that you haven't got any dig . . .

BRIAN (*Grabbing hold of Dave's arm and twisting it behind his back*) Oh no? Haven't I?

DAVE Let go!

BRIAN (*Twisting more*) Haven't I?

(*Dave gives a huge pull and breaks away but Brian grabs hold of him again. A fight — half-serious, half in fun — breaks out. The rest of the class are so interested in what is going on that they do not notice Michael walk into the classroom.*)

MICHAEL Is Gary Tait here?

(*Everyone freezes. Then, as they realise that it is a boy and not a teacher, they relax.*)

GARY Yes. What d'you want?

MICHAEL Mr Robinson said I should look for you.

BRIAN Terrett! *Michael* Terrett — that's your name, isn't it?

MICHAEL That's right.

BRIAN I know you — Harton High School — that's right, isn't it?

GARY What is this?

BRIAN Yes, I know you all right.

MICHAEL Well, I don't know you.

BRIAN What happened up there, then? Get the boot did you?

MICHAEL What are you talking about?

Follow-up Activities

The Traveller

Talking in Role (pair work)

A, B and C go home and tell someone at home about what happened.

D speaks to his father or mother on the phone and explains what happened.

Discussion Points
Do we often judge other people by their clothing? Should we? Do we expect to be judged by what we wear?

Good Neighbours

Talking in Role (pair work)
Mr Selby complains to the local council and they send round an official, who talks to A, B, C, D and E about what has been happening.

Discussion Points
How far should we go in changing our way of life to fit in with neighbours? What is your opinion of the way the parents reacted to David's and Maria's news? Could the scene have had a different ending?

Interview

Writing in Role
A and B write reports on the two applicants.
C and D describe the interview in their diaries.

Discussion Points
What did the interviewers think of the two applicants? Whom would they have chosen for the job and why? What did the applicants think of the interview? Were the interviewers fair?

It's a Secret

Writing
The reporter writes a story for the local paper.

Discussion Points
How much of Peter's real story came out in the scene? Was he right to try to conceal it? What would you have done? What do you think of the reporter's part in all this?

The New Boy

Some Points to Think About
Does Brian really know something about Michael, or is he mistaken (or fooling)? If he does, what is Michael's secret and

how does Brian know about it? How does Michael react — is he worried, or unconcerned? Why has he changed schools? What are the characters of Brian, Michael, Gary and the rest?

Section 5
Work

When you start work you find that not only do you make new friends and develop new relationships, but also some of your existing relationships change.

Your position in the family begins to change. Instead of just *taking out* of the family, you can begin to make a real contribution, especially by adding to the family income. You have greater responsibility outside the home and think, perhaps, that you should be treated differently inside it as well. At work you meet new people with different attitudes to life and you have to learn to fit in. You may even find yourself in conflict with those you work with, or those you work *for*.

On the other hand, you may find that while you are doing well at work, it does not satisfy you. You have ambitions to do something better or more interesting. Why should people be condemned to spend the best part of every day, every week, every year, doing something that they find boring and repetitive? Does the world have to be like that? William Morris once said that in a good society anybody who wanted to start a factory should be asked two questions:

> *"First, will the thing being produced be useful to the world? Second, will the making of it give healthy and pleasurable occupation to the makers?"*

Those words were written about a hundred years ago, but they are still important today. Try applying them to some of the jobs that people do in your locality and see what answers you get.

Breadwinner

Characters

A — Father or mother
B — Son or daughter

Situation

B is seventeen and has been working for a year at a local

factory. He/she earns a good wage and makes a small but regular contribution to the family budget. B keeps most of the week's wages, however, and has been saving steadily since starting work.

Setting

The living room of their house.

Organisation

Cast the parts.
Arrange your working space.
Read your separate instructions, but do not discuss them.
A – 36
B – 62

Starting Point

It is about 6 pm on a Friday evening, when B comes in from work. A is sitting in the living room, reading the paper.

Generation Gap

Characters

People working in the office of the Norwich and Norfolk Insurance Company.

A – Mr Waylett, the manager, aged about 55
B – Miss Clarke, the senior secretary, with responsibility for running the 'outer office' and the discipline of the junior staff.
C – Anne Richards, a shorthand typist, who has worked in the office for six months.
D – The junior clerk who does all the odd jobs. (Name and sex to be suited to the person taking the part.)

Situation

In the past the Norwich and Norfolk has been a settled and happy office, but recently there has been a rapid turnover of junior staff. It is now the time of year when holiday dates have to be decided. Only one of the four characters may be on holiday at a time.

Setting

The outer office. There are two doors, one leading to a

corridor, the other into Mr Waylett's office. Tables and chairs with typewriters etc.

Organisation
Cast the parts.
Arrange your working area.
Read your separate instructions, but do not discuss them.

A — 9	C — 31
B — 58	D — 48

Starting Point
It is just *after* the mid-morning coffee break. Anne Richards and the junior clerk are still drinking their coffee. At the same time Anne is doing her nails and the junior clerk is reading a magazine. Miss Clarke comes in with the holiday list to take to Anne Richards. Mr Waylett is in his office.

Troublemaker

Characters
A — Personnel Manager
B — Worker

Situation
A and B work for a long-established company manufacturing gardening and agricultural chemicals. In the past the company has been very successful but recently, partly because of strikes and partly because of management and financial problems, it has begun to lose money. A is a newcomer to the firm, but B has worked there for years.

Setting
A's office. A table and two chairs.

Organisation
Cast the parts.
Organise your working area.
Read your separate instructions, but do not discuss them.
A — 45
B — 20

Starting Point
The section that B works in has just started working again after a lightning strike to protest about working conditions. It is 11.15 am and A is sitting working in his office, when B walks in without knocking.

Ambition

Characters
A — aged 18, works in a car factory
B — his fiancee. (They have been engaged for three months.)
C — his father, works in a garage
D — his mother.

Situation
A spends nearly all the money he earns on having very expensive lessons to be a racing driver. He recently had a very serious accident and was lucky to escape with bruises and a broken arm. Both B and C have always supported A in his ambition to be a racing driver. So far D has not really committed herself.

Setting
The dining room in A's house. A table and four chairs.

Organisation
Cast the parts.
Arrange your working area.
Read your separate instructions, but do not discuss them.

A — **66**	C — **44**
B — **3**	D — **28**

Starting Point
It is the day that A has gone to the hospital to have the plaster taken off his arm. It is tea time and B, C and D have already started their tea. A comes in.

Safety Guard

Setting
A production line. Two girls, Mary and Yvonne are operating a machine that wraps cakes in cellophane. It has a safety

guard which has to be operated every time the machine is used. As they work, they talk.

YVONNE Went over to Dave's last night.
MARY Oh yes? We went to the pictures.
YVONNE What did you see?
MARY Wasn't much good — 'Bruce Lee Lives On'.
YVONNE I don't like those films.
MARY Me neither, but Pete's mad on all that stuff.
YVONNE Look out — here comes Mussolini.
(Harry, the foreman, comes up to them.)
HARRY Do you two girls ever stop talking?
MARY I don't know what you mean, Mr Jones.
HARRY I bet. And how many times have I told you to put the guard down *every time* you work that machine?
YVONNE But it slows everything down so much. You have to lift it up to get the cake out and then put it down again when you've got the next one in —
MARY And while you're doing that another three cakes have piled up to be wrapped.
HARRY If you didn't yack so much there'd be no problem. If you get your fingers chopped off don't blame me.
(Harry goes.)
YVONNE Male chauvinist pig. Anyway, as I was saying, I went up to Dave's . . .
MARY Has he got that new bike yet?
YVONNE No, he's still waiting for it.
MARY He's been waiting for ages.
YVONNE Yes — nearly four months now. He says if they don't deliver it soon, he's — LOOK OUT MARY!!!

Follow-up Activities

Breadwinner

Talking in Role (pair work)

The two parents discuss B's attitude.
B tells a friend about what happened.

Discussion Points

When you get a job how much do you expect to contribute

to the family income? How much do you expect your parents to influence this? Do you think B is being selfish or reasonable? What about A?

Generation Gap

Writing in Role

A — write a report on the members of your staff for Head Office.
B — Write a report on Anne Richards and the junior clerk, for Mr Waylett.
C/D Write a letter to a friend, telling him/her about what happened and what you think of the office.

Troublemaker

Talking in Role (pair work)

A talks to the foreman about B.
B tells a friend about his conversation with A.

Discussion Points

Are conflicts like this inevitable in a factory? What are the reasons behind them? Could they be avoided? If so, how?

Ambition

Writing in Role

Write a description of the day that A had his accident, as seen by your character.

Discussion Points

How far should A take notice of what the others say? Why?

Safety Guard

It will probably help in developing this scene, if you begin by concentrating on the physical aspects of the setting. How and where are the two girls standing? What actions do they perform? How do they do them — energetically? automatically? lazily? sloppily? What happens when Yvonne shouts out 'LOOK OUT MARY!!!'?

Section 6
Larger Situations

The situations in this section are longer and more complicated than those in the rest of the book. Apart from this, they are similar to the other situations and you can work on them in the same way.

The first situation, *Happy Family . . .* examines what happens when a young married couple are forced to live with their parents in a house that is not big enough. Tensions arise and, as you will see, these lead to serious conflicts.

The second, *The Walls*, concerns something that happened some years ago in Oxford. The situation is really asking the question, *when someone buys a house, just what are they entitled to?* Do they, for example, get the exclusive right to the use of their own street? Can they keep out people they do not like? In fact — how private should private property be?

The third situation, *Squatters* continues this theme. Some people believe that it is wrong for very wealthy people to own a number of houses (some of which are left empty) while poor people have nowhere to live. So they act according to their beliefs and occupy such empty houses as a demonstration. The owner of such a house, who has paid good money for it, naturally believes that it is his to do as he likes with. Who is right?

Happy Family

Characters

A — Anne Stanford, the mother, aged 39. She has a part-time job, helping out at a local primary school. She is also an agent for a cosmetic firm, going from door to door taking and delivering orders. She is rather houseproud.

B — George Stanford, the father, aged 47. He is a senior cashier at a bank in the city. He is also chairman of the local operatic and dramatic society and this takes up a lot of his spare time.

C — Peter Stanford, their son, aged 20. He had been studying electronics at a local polytechnic. Shortly after starting the course, he married Helen, who was a student there. The following year she had a baby, so he had to leave college and get a job as a TV repairer to earn enough money to support Helen and the baby.

D — Helen Stanford, Peter's wife, aged 22. She now lives at home and looks after their baby daughter Sarah.

Situation

Because of the severe local housing shortage, when Peter and Helen married they had to move in with his parents. Now although they have a child, they are still living there because they cannot find anywhere else that they can afford.

Setting

For both scenes you will need two adjoining rooms: kitchen and living room. The kitchen is large and is used as a dining room as well.

Organisation

Cast the parts.

Arrange your working space.

Now read your separate instructions, but do not discuss them.

A — **37**	C — **25**
B — **11**	D — **50**

Think about your character and his or her feelings about the general situation before starting work on *Scene One*.

Scene One

Anne has said that she will babysit while Peter and Helen go to the pictures (for the first time in months). George has gone to a rehearsal at the operatic and dramatic society. All three of them are due back at around 11 pm. It is now nearly midnight and Anne is still sitting on her own, waiting.

Preparation

George
Peter and Helen } Decide why you are late, but don't tell Anne.

Anne — Decide how you feel about all this.

Starting Point
Anne is sitting alone in the living room, and then George comes in. After a few moments Peter and Helen come in.

Scene Two
It is Friday evening. George, Anne and Helen are sitting having tea. They have started without Peter, because he is late. For different reasons they are all a bit irritable.

Preparation
George, Anne and Helen — decide why you are annoyed.
Peter — read role instruction **41**.

Starting Point
George, Anne and Helen are sitting at the table.
Peter comes in.

The Walls

In the early 1930s, some land to the north of the city of Oxford became available for building. The Council used half of it to build Council houses on, and sold the other half to a development company, who built a private housing estate. The Council estate was known as the *Cutteslowe Estate* and the private one as the *Urban Housing Estate*. They were very different. The Cutteslowe Estate was used to rehouse people from slum areas of the city and most of them were working class. The Urban Housing Estate was for people who bought their own houses (owner-occupiers), who were mostly middle class. The two estates were right next to each other and the quickest route from Cutteslowe to the main road which led to the city centre went through the middle of the Urban Estate . . . If you didn't go this way, then you had to make a big detour round the outside of the Urban Estate.

While the estates were being built, the Council planned to join up two roads through the Urban estate, linking Cutteslowe with the main road. When the estates were completed, the company building the private estate enclosed it and blocked off the two roads, by building high walls across them:

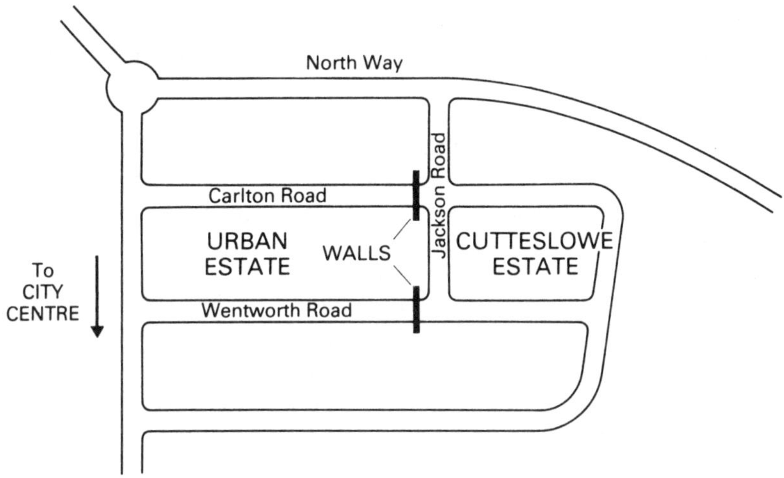

The company insisted that the City Council had said that they could make the roads private in this way and also said that the Council had promised that they would not use the Cutteslowe estate for rehousing people from the slums, which they had then done. Despite protests and demonstrations by the people of Cutteslowe and strenuous efforts by the Council, the walls remained in place, blocking off the roads, until 1959, over twenty years after they had been put up.

Scene One
The walls have been built. There have been protests by the people from the Cutteslowe Estate. As a result, the City Council have agreed to a public meeting about the problem.

Characters
Group A — The Council Housing Committee
Group B — The Press
Group C — Representatives of the builders of the Urban Estate
Group D — Families living on the Urban Estate
Group E — Families living on the Cutteslowe Estate

One person: The Independent Chairman of the Meeting.

Because so many different characters are involved, you will probably find that you have to use the whole class or drama group for this scene.

Setting
A local hall, with a platform at one end for the main speakers.

Organisation
Arrange the working area, with a table and chairs at one end (the platform) and enough chairs in the main part of the 'hall'. Cast the parts and arrange for the different groups to sit together, but separate from each other.
Now read the instructions for your group.

A — **47**	D — **23**
B — **6**	E — **35**
C — **38**	Chairman — **2**

Now, in preparation for the public meeting, each group should discuss separately what will happen at that meeting.

Starting Point
The Chairman enters the hall, ready to start the public meeting. Then, in their groups, those attending gradually come in and sit down. When they are all there, the Chairman starts the meeting.

Scene Two
After the public meeting, a radio interviewer gathers together a number of people who have been at the meeting and asks them some questions about what happened, and their feelings about it.

Characters
Radio interviewer
Cutteslowe resident
Urban resident
Council official

Setting
Four chairs round a table on which there is a microphone. If you can use a tape recorder to record the discussion, so much the better.

Organisation
Cast the parts.
Arrange the working area.

Before starting the interview, spend some time thinking about the meeting that took place in *Scene One* and how your character thinks about it. You are probably playing a member of a different group from the one you were in for *Scene One*, so this needs some thought and imagination to be really effective.

Starting Point
The interviewer makes a few introductory remarks about the public meeting and then starts by asking one of the others a question.

Squatters

MILLIONAIRE MOVES OUT . . .
. . . SQUATTERS MOVE IN

Last night, only hours after millionaire chainstore-owner Marcus Grand moved out of his luxury penthouse flat in London's fashionable Mayfair, the squatters moved in.

Millionaire Grand had left London and arrived for an indefinite stay in Guernsey, tax-haven of the wealthy, before he heard the news. '*I've been in touch with my lawyers,*' he told me on the phone, 'and they are taking any necessary action. After all it is still my house and I shall be wanting to go back there eventually. It's the only house I actually own. This place belongs to a friend, it isn't mine.' (*This place* is a 16 bedroom luxury villa with private beach, swimming pool and marina.)

Later I managed to speak to the squatters' leader, Dave Gerrish. He told me that the squatters are all members of LAP (Londoners Against Poverty). Their aim is to highlight the predicament of London's homeless. '*It is obscene,*' said 23-year-old Gerrish, 'that a house like this should lie empty while there are people living five to a room in some parts of London. We aim to stay here as long as we have to in order to get justice for the homeless.' I pointed out that Marcus Grand intended to take legal action to get the squatters out. 'There is no way he'll get us out – short of physical violence,' stated Gerrish. 'And if the owner wishes to return to his house?' 'He won't – he's too busy tax-dodging in the Channel Islands. But if he does . . . we'll have to wait and see what happens.'

Characters

Group A — Dave Gerrish
The squatters

Group B — Marcus Grand
His wife Suzanne
His two lawyers

Situation
Grand has returned suddenly from Guernsey. He has already tried to get back into his apartment, with the help of bailiffs and policemen, but has failed. Now he has sent the police away and the squatters have agreed to let him, his wife, and two lawyers in to the apartment to talk things over.

Setting
The main living area of Grand's luxury apartment.

Organisation
Cast the parts.
Arrange the working area.
Read your separate instructions and then hold separate discussions of Group A and Group B about how to approach the situation. Do not listen to what the other group are saying.
Group A — 72
Group B — 43

Starting Point
When both groups are ready the discussion between them can begin.

Follow-up Activity

Role play in pairs
A TV interviewer conducts a rather hostile interview with each of the people involved in the discussions inside Grand's apartment. He doesn't seem to believe a lot of what he is told and keeps on insisting that 'the public have a right to know the truth'.

Section 7
Roles

1 There has been a lot of trouble recently with young people 'on the road'. You think that this young man looks all right, and you would like to help him. You really think, though, that the best thing would be for him to go back home.

2 This whole business is most unfortunate. Still, it is done now, and the Development Company seem to be in the right legally if not morally. Of course no *action* can be taken as a result of this public meeting, but it will give people a chance to air their feelings. What you, as Chairman, must make sure of, is that it does not turn into a shouting match. Everyone can have a say, but each has a right to be heard.

3 You are glad to see A back. You want to persuade him to give up this idea of being a racing driver because it is dangerous and expensive. You would like to start saving some money so that the two of you can get married and settle down.

4 You envy A's life as a student and you hope that you will do well enough at school to be able to go to university yourself.

5 The bike is not in fact yours. You do a part-time job at the local bike shop and you managed to persuade the manager to let you have the bike just for the evening. You promised the manager faithfully that you would look after it and that you wouldn't let anyone else ride it. Just for fun you pretended to the others that it was *your* bike. It would be embarrassing now to have to admit that it isn't. You are covered by your own third-party insurance, but it does *not* cover the damage to the bike.

6 It seems that both the Council and the Development Company (the builders) have gone back on their word. On the other hand,
a) why are the Urban Estate people so insistent on shutting themselves off like this? Is it because they are snobs or is there

some deeper, more important reason?
b) why are the Cutteslowe residents so determined to have access through the Urban Estate? Is it just a matter of their convenience? Or is there also a principle at stake?
The public have a right to know — especially the ratepayers of Oxford who have paid for the building of the Cutteslowe Estate. Decide at your meeting whom you want to question and what you want to ask them.

7 You have just been offered a free holiday in New York, through a contact of your father's. If you are to go, it must be next week. This means not only cancelling your Norfolk Broads holiday, but also asking for your money back, so that you can have some spending money in New York. This will be difficult because you know how much the others have been looking forward to their Broads holiday.

8 You are very concerned about the Lees and the effect they are having on the house and the neighbourhood. To call them anti-social is an understatement. You cannot make up your mind whether to make an official complaint about them to the council or to start looking for a new house. You were just settling down to read in the garden, after a hard day's work when Lee started hammering.

9 On the holiday list, you have chosen the first half of June. Miss Clarke has chosen the second half.
You have recently been told by Head Office that:
a) they are concerned that your office is inefficient;
b) they think you are losing too many junior staff.
Therefore you feel that you must try to make the office more efficient without putting up the backs of the junior staff. You think that Miss Richards is a bad influence on the junior clerk.
Note: You should choose a moment to enter the outer office, and have some reason for doing so.

10 You arrived at the club early, and as you got there you noticed someone climbing over a wall at the back of the club. A number of windows had been smashed. You telephoned the police and they arrived surprisingly quickly. You told them what had happened, and, after looking at the damage, they left again. You then spoke to the club leader, who arrived while you were talking to the police. You went into his room and told

him what had happened. *Do not join in the scene with the others until they tell you to.*

11 You are very enthusiastic about your work with the operatic and dramatic society and think that if you had had the chance you might have been able to take it up professionally. It is a continuing disappointment that your family does not share your enthusiasm, but you still manage to take your wife out a fair bit at weekends. Your work at the office is routine but responsible. Your attitude towards the presence of Peter and Helen in the house is that it is a pity but cannot be helped. They don't get in the way too much and you expect that they will be able to get a place of their own fairly soon.

12 You are beginning to feel hemmed in by life at home. A has been nagging you and prying into your private life. On the other hand you have been feeling irritable and tired, too, so maybe it is partly your fault. You have decided to try to make things up and so have bought A a present. You have hidden it in a suitcase, which you have stuck under your bed. You were just getting the present out to wrap it up, when A came into your room — snooping again?

13 Your parents have told you that you are under no circumstances to see B and C again because they disapprove of the way they behave. (Decide what your feelings are about this.) You have decided to see B and C again — maybe for the last time, or perhaps because you have decided to ignore what your parents said. (Decide which of these it is before you begin the scene.)

14 The work you were doing in the army wasn't secret at all. You were in the Signals, but pretended that what you were doing was secret, just to impress your family. Then, just before you were due to come home on leave, you were out one evening with a girl you had met in a bar. The bar was attacked by terrorists. When the attack started you told the girl to run and did so yourself. She didn't escape, and was injured. When this was discovered by your Commanding Officer you were sent back to England while further enquiries were made. Naturally you don't want your parents or fiancee to know anything about this.

15 You borrowed the bike. You were only going to take it down the road a bit, but it was too heavy for you, and you came off. You were only going very slowly, so you weren't hurt, and the bike was not damaged. Unfortunately as you got up, a car came up behind and hit the bike, which was still lying in the road. The car was almost unmarked and, after giving you a piece of his mind, the driver went off. You are a bit scared of A.

16 You have the chance of getting two tickets for an event you would give almost anything to attend. (Decide what it is — cup final, pop concert or whatever.) In order to make sure of the tickets, though, you need another £2. You must have the money today and B is the only person you can think of who is likely to be able to lend it to you — B always seems to have plenty of money. In any case B has always been fairly easy-going about lending things — you still have a couple of B's records that you borrowed ages ago. On the other hand you have offered the spare ticket to someone else (decide who) and it would be very embarrassing if B found out, as you and B have been friends for so long.

17 Your parents have had a long talk with you about B. They think that you are seeing her far too often and that this was the reason why you did so badly in the exams last year. They have told you that if you want to stay on into the sixth form you must stop seeing B so often. You know that B is rather critical of your parents, but you think that they are probably right. You have to tell her today that you can only see her once a week during term time. You aren't looking forward to it.

18 You are annoyed that A is so late, and suspicious. It is not like him to behave in this way.

19 You think it is important to get someone who is efficient, hard-working and, if necessary, ruthless. What they look like, and whether they are 'nice to know' have got nothing to do with it.

20 Recently you have been finding your work very frustrating indeed. There is a new foreman who seems to keep on picking on you and making sarcastic remarks and criticisms. The machinery keeps on breaking down, the whole section is falling behind its production targets and the foreman seems to be blaming it all on you. You've had enough — you've worked at this firm for over ten years and this is all the thanks you get. You've decided to have the whole thing out with the Personnel Manager. After all he was the one who appointed the new foreman and the two of them seem to be great friends.

21 You have recently been going out with a friend of the opposite sex. You have not told B about this — mainly because you know it would cause all sorts of problems and you don't want to hurt B's feelings. So you have pretended, when you have a date, that you are going out babysitting.

22 You are looking forward to this holiday very much. About a fortnight ago you were offered the chance of a very cheap trip to Greece, but you turned it down: partly because you were looking forward to this Broads holiday; and partly because you didn't want to let your friends down.

23 You have all spent your own money on your new homes on the Urban Estate. Some of you have spent the savings of many years to do this. You have had to make sacrifices to buy a place of your own and with it a little peace and quiet. Now these Cutteslowe people want to come tramping through your private estate as a short cut. They have not had to make the sacrifices that you have and they are not the kind of people you would wish to mix with socially. At your meeting decide how you can best put across your point of view.

24 You have been offered the chance of a very good job in Australia. It means promotion and a lot more money. In order to be given the job you have had to *say* that you are emigrating (going out and not coming back) but you know that if things go wrong and you don't like it, you will soon be able to afford the fare back. Even if you do like it, you are not planning to spend more than four or five years out there. Still it is going to be a big surprise for A and you *must* tell A this weekend, because you are due to leave for Australia in three weeks' time.

25 Things are not going too well. Your mother appears to be getting increasingly irritable and you never seem to be able to get through to your father. The work you are doing is quite well paid, but dull. The trouble is that you can't see how to get a better job without qualifications. At the moment you go out once a week to an evening class and you are trying to do a correspondence course, but, with the baby and everything, it isn't easy.

26 Your background is that you have just spent three years at drama school and then you did a bit of office training. You are confident and relaxed and not only find it easy to get on with people but you positively enjoy meeting new people.

27 You think that A has been getting too big for his boots recently and needs taking down a peg or two.

28 You are delighted to see A back. Now he's had this accident, he will stop all this silly car racing business and settle down. You have been finding it difficult to make ends meet recently and you need more housekeeping money. A has contributed almost nothing to the family budget because of paying for his lessons. Perhaps if he gives up the lessons he will be able to help you out.

29 You have left school and have a year to spare before going to college. With your parents' approval you have decided to hitch-hike round Britain. Unfortunately today you lost your wallet, containing all your money, and you have nowhere to spend the night, and no money with which to buy food. You can get some money from your parents by phoning them tomorrow, when they will have returned from holiday. So you need to borrow some money to last you until tomorrow.

30 There is no doubt in your mind that you should take the money back to the old man who gave you the jacket. He can't have meant to leave the money in the pocket. If B won't agree to go back with you, you are determined to go and tell the old man on your own — it is your duty.

31 You *must* have your holiday in the first fortnight of July because you have already arranged a holiday on the Welsh coast. The only other possibility is the first half of June, when some friends who are going to Brittany have offered you a place in their car. You think that Mr Waylett is a drip, although Miss Clarke is all right, if a bit old-fashioned. You are fed up with things in this stuffy office.

32 Now that A has finished at university, you expect him/her to settle down quickly, find a job and start to bring some money into the house. You have not objected to paying to keep A at university but it will be good to have a little extra to spend on the house and the family as a whole. Still, A has always been fairly sensible and you expect that he/she will settle down to proper work quickly.

33 You are glad to have Peter back because you are so proud of him, although from the look of him he needs a good rest and some decent food. Then he can settle down at home with you for a while.

34 You know that it was D who took the bike, because you saw him, but he doesn't know that you saw. You have more or less decided not to tell A — that's D's business.

35 You really cannot understand the attitude of the people on the Urban Housing Estate. After all, everyone is supposed to be equal and all men have a right to a place to live. Those walls have been put there to separate off the Urban Estate people, presumably because they think that they are better than you. As a result it takes twice as long to get to the shops as it would if you could go straight along Wentworth Road or Carlton Road. At your meeting decide on the main points that you would like to make when you go to the public meeting.

36 Now that B seems to have really settled down at work, you are beginning to feel that you can rely on 'that little bit extra' coming in each week. If B could manage to give you just a little bit more each week, you would be able to afford to build a small home extension, which would make the house more comfortable. You have decided to ask B about this today.

37 You are becoming increasingly dissatisfied with your life. Your husband seems to spend all his spare time at the operatic and dramatic society and rarely takes you out anywhere. As a result you have to spend a lot of time at home with Helen. You do not get on very well with her and in addition she is lazy and never seems to do her share of the housework. You think that your life should be more than this.

38 When you built the Urban Estate, you promised the people who bought the houses that it would be a high-class residential area. The Council promised you that they would not use the Cutteslowe estate for rehousing low grade families from the slums. They broke their promise. You would be letting down the people who bought the houses if you were to remove the walls. It would mean that the Cutteslowe people could use the Urban Estate, a private estate, as a short cut to the shops. At your meeting decide how you should approach the public meeting. How best can you protect the interests of the Urban Estate people?

39 Secretly you have been going out with Maria for three months, although you know that your parents would disapprove. You think your parents are stuffy and snobbish about the Lees. Now you and Maria have decided that you want to get married. You want to tell your parents about it and introduce Maria to them properly. She is waiting inside the house for you to take her into the garden, but first you want to speak to your parents on your own and explain things to them.

40 B has been secretive lately and you are worried about this. You are also concerned about the fact that B has been coming in late in the evenings. You want to have a talk with B about all this, so you go to B's room. When you open the door your first impression is that B has decided to leave home secretly.

41 You have just got the sack. Before entering the scene, decide why, how it happened, and how you feel about it.

42 You don't have a very high opinion of B — you think he's always trying to stir up trouble.

43 As you expected, these squatters are the usual crowd of students, lefties and hangers-on. You cannot use physical force to evict the squatters. The police will not be able to take direct action either. Until you have a court order, it is impossible to have these people evicted. It is disgusting that they should have invaded the flat and taken it over in this way, and you are very angry indeed. But all you can do, because of the laws of the country, is to try to persuade them that it is in their best interests to leave. After all, when the court order comes through they can be removed by force. They can't win in the long run, so why don't they go quietly now?

44 You are glad to see A back. You think he should now give up thoughts of being a racing driver. You have watched him driving on the track once or twice recently and from your experience (you are a keen motor racing fan) you don't think he has what it takes. This recent accident confirmed your opinion.

45 The section of the firm where B works has had a lot of trouble and unofficial strikes in the past few months. You like B and you think he has always been a conscientious worker, but someone has told you that he is a Communist agitator and is at the back of all these stoppages. You don't really believe it and are thinking of asking him along to your office to talk things over. He might even be able to give you some idea of the real cause of the trouble.

46 Since A became a student, he/she has changed. A used to be neat and tidy, considerate towards others, hard-working and quiet. Now A has become scruffy, careless, thoughtless and selfish. You are glad that this university nonsense is over and A can settle down to a proper job and to being a normal human being again.

47 It seems that the building firm are probably right when they say that you cannot force them to knock the walls down. On the other hand you are under pressure from the Cutteslowe people to do something about the matter and the builders did promise originally that they would allow access through the Urban Estate. At your meeting decide how you want the public meeting to go. Remember that the Chairman is independent and not necessarily on your side.

48 You *must* have your holiday in the first fortnight of July because that is when you and some friends have planned your holiday together in the Lake District. However, it is just possible that it could be switched to the second half of June if you did something about it today. You think Mr Waylett is all right, if rather vague, but Miss Clarke is a bossy old dragon, and you are thinking of looking somewhere else for a job.

49 You have said that A is not to see B and C again under any circumstances. You think they are having a bad influence on A. You are out shopping in the town and are very surprised to see A sitting in the cafe talking to B and C. You have decided to go in and speak to A straight away.
Note: Give the scene in the cafe time to get started, before entering.

50 Life is very difficult for you, living in another person's house. The baby is fine and you are very happily married to Peter *but* Peter's mother is constantly on at you about the house. His father is never in and when he does come home, all he can talk about is that amateur dramatic society he belongs to. Because of this and the fact that the house is really overcrowded, the evenings are awful. You and Peter never seem to have any time alone together and when you do, all he wants to do is study.

51 The Selbys are snobbish prigs and most unpleasant in the way that they ignore you and your family. You are glad that no one in your family is anything like them.

52 There was some trouble at the match. You don't normally get involved, but on this occasion you could not avoid it. A group of the other side's supporters set on you and a friend of yours, and you just had to defend yourselves. Then the police came along, the others all ran away and you were arrested. Now the police say that you must attend court on Monday. You will have to tell your parents.

53 You have had an anonymous phone call to say that this young man is back from service in Belfast and that he has been mixed up in some very odd business about a girl and some terrorists. When you asked the caller to give you more details, all he would say was, 'Ask him why he left his girl to the gunment.'

54 You are not really looking forward much to this holiday. You are beginning to find the others in the group boring and you have started to go around with new and more interesting friends. Still, you said you would go and you won't let the others down.

55 You have just found out that when A goes out 'baby-sitting', he/she is in fact going out with a boyfriend/girlfriend. A has not said anything about this to you at all. Decide how you feel about it — hurt, angry, amused, or what? Then when A comes in, speak to him/her about it.

56 You have decided that B is likely to stay in London for a considerable time. Most of your friends have retired and moved away from Coventry, so there is little point in staying there yourself. So you have sold your house (the one that this scene takes place in) and are negotiating to buy a bungalow near where B lives in London. You have got to be out of your present house in three weeks' time, so it is essential that you tell B straight away what you have done.

57 The main job that the Assistant Personnel Manager will have to do is meet the people working for Partysound. It is essential, therefore, that you should appoint someone who is confident and relaxed and can converse easily with all sorts of different people. You don't want someone who is efficient and ruthless like A or half the firm will be out on strike in five minutes.

58 On the holiday list you have chosen the second half of June, while Mr Waylett has the first. You respect Mr Waylett, but you think he is too soft with the juniors so it is your job to be firm with them. You are glad that you have recently been able to get rid of a number of inefficient juniors. You think that the junior clerk is a bad influence on Miss Richards.

59 You wanted a chance to talk to A about two records you lent him/her six weeks ago. They are two of your favourites and you think it is about time that you had them back. You suspect that A has not been looking after them and may even have damaged or lost them, which would certainly explain why you have not had them back.

60 You think that your husband does go on rather about the Lee family but tonight when you heard Mr Lee making all that noise, even you got angry.

61 Your letter says that you have got a good second-class degree (well above average), good enough for you to be able to stay on at the university for at least another year to do an

MA. This is what you want to do, because university life appeals to you and you have a lot of friends still at the university. In addition the more qualifications you have, the better the job you will be able to find in the end. Of course your parents will have to continue to help you financially, but they have enough money to be able to do that.

62 You have put up with your present job for exactly a year and it has bored you stiff. You are not treated as a human being, just as an anonymous 'employee'. You have had as much as you can stand and have decided to pack it in. You've managed to save quite a bit and now you think you'll take a month's holiday, touring around a bit, before deciding what to do next. You have asked for your cards, and now you must tell A about your decision.

63 You like A a lot, but you think he is weak-willed. As for his parents, you know they don't like you and would give anything for him to give you up. If only A would stand up for his rights!

64 You are glad to see Peter back because you missed him so much. You have noticed that there is something odd about his behaviour, although you cannot quite work out what it is. You hope that the two of you will be able to get married as soon as possible, so that you can get him away from his mother who fusses too much.

65 You like A, but you think that his parents have some rather odd ideas. (Decide the details of this for yourself, before the scene begins.)

66 You want to start having lessons again as soon as the doctor says you can, probably in about a fortnight if you do the exercises he has given you. You will, however, need to borrow about £20 because you have lost money while you have been off sick. If you can't get the money, it means that you will have to stop the lessons until you have earned enough to start again. You think perhaps your mother could lend you the £20.

67 You have been looking forward to this holiday for months. It has meant scraping together every last penny and you won't have a lot of spare money to spend, but you know it's going to be worth it and you have already started planning in your mind what you are going to do.

68 You have three good A levels and a diploma in business studies. You are working, very successfully, in the office of a very large firm of travel agents. You are generally considered to be efficient and tough but perhaps a bit curt in conversations with people.

69 You have just heard that the police are round at Dave's house and that he is in trouble. You know that A is in the club leader's room. You think he may have informed the police about Dave.

70 You are angry with A because you had made him his favourite tea and it was all wasted. Now all you want to do is go to bed, because it has been a long day and you are tired.

71 There has been a lot of trouble recently in the town with long-haired teenagers. You think it is time that the police did something about it so that respectable people can walk through the streets at night without being terrified or mugged.

72 You are determined not to give in. Grand can stay if he likes, but he's not getting you out. Try to explain to him exactly why you are there and just how serious you are. Perhaps you could even persuade him to do something for LAP. Decide what he could do to help.

73 You did not even know that A had left the bike outside your house — you thought he'd taken it back home. You hurt your face just before tea when you were playing with your younger brother. (Decide exactly *how* it happened.)

74 Your family has been very hard up ever since your father lost his job. This money would mean that you could buy a present for your mother. It's her birthday next week and at the moment it doesn't look as if she is going to receive much in the way of presents. There isn't really anything wrong with taking the money. After all the old man did *give* you the jacket and could easily spare the money. He must be very rich, living in a house like that.

75 Secretly you have been going out with David Selby for three months. One of the things you admire about him is that he is so calm and quiet compared with your family. Now the two of you have decided that you want to get married. He wants to introduce you to his parents. He has left you to wait inside their house while he goes into the garden to tell them.